THE GREAT ANIMATOR

For Anne

THE GREAT ANIMATOR

ROY MARSHALL

with best wishes

Roy Marshall

Shoestring Press

Printed by imprintdigital
Upton Pyne, Exeter
www.digital.imprint.co.uk

Typesetting and cover design by narrator
www.narrator.me.uk
info@narrator.me.uk
033 022 300 39

Published by Shoestring Press
19 Devonshire Avenue, Beeston, Nottingham, NG9 1BS
(0115) 925 1827
www.shoestringpress.co.uk

First published 2017
© Copyright: Roy Marshall
© Copyright cover image: Ayo Byron

The moral right of the author has been asserted.

ISBN 978-1-910323-78-6

ACKNOWLEDGEMENTS

Thanks are due to the editors of the following publications where versions of some of these poems have appeared. *Ambit, Antiphon, And Other Poems, The Butcher's Dog, Clear Poetry, Hinterland, Lucifer, Magma, Matter, New Walk, Poetry Wales, Proletarian Poetry, Poetry Spotlight, Stand, The Compass, The Interpreter's House, The Morning Star, The North, The Rialto, The Stare's Nest, The High Window, The Manchester Review* and anthologies *More Raw Material, Millstone Grit* and *Vanguard Editions 2 Poetry Anthology.*

Other poems were awarded prizes in the Alan Sillitoe, Nottingham Open, Ver Open Poetry Competition, East Midlands Aurora Prize, Swindon Festival and Wenlock International poetry competitions. A version of 'Night Swimming' appeared on a beermat as a winner of the 2014 Poems on a Beermat competition.

Special thanks to my editor John Lucas.

Thanks also to Rachel and Alex, Susannah Evans, Noel Williams, John Foggin, Keith Hutson, James Giddings, Maria Taylor, Rory Waterman, Jo Shapcott and Richard Skinner.

For Alan and Cathy

CONTENTS

I

THE HORSES

In the first bright slew of laughter and bedclothes
we hear them, and cars slowing to pass,
the drifting talk of their riders.
They clop through gathering dark
as lights come on and the baby kicks
and dreams inside you. Hooves break
the skin of our sleep, wake us to green shoots
or rusted leaves, to shoe prints in early frost,
a puddled road and soft scatterings.
The boy grows tall and oversleeps
as we lie tangled or back to back,
while the phone brings news
of a slipping away, a collapse
into nearly nothing. Blossom is blown
to blizzard, blackbirds return
to nest in clematis. But always
we hear horses; though we never know
their barreled flanks, the sway
and tilt of a saddled back
as they trot through the days
of promise, arrival, exit.

ESPRESSO

Who knew that the child, screwing up his face
at that first sip, would find this a necessity;
the aroma suffusing mornings where a radio plays
extracts of bombing runs, gunshots outside a café
as he stands by the humming machine's twin streams,
flicking the switch when the last drops pock the crema.
He might down it on the spot, or sit on the step to watch
sparrows dust-bathe. Often, he'll carry the cup to the room
where he pours memories into a book, looking up to find
his reflection floating in a black sky. Maybe if all the cups
he'd drunk were stood in line they'd stretch to Ethiopia
where the kaffa plant grew among the first humans.
His heart, once as easily excited by this dark syrup
as by a lover's touch, has grown steady, accustomed.

HERON

He's as unexpected
as royalty

on this river-less estate.
A rook sees him off

and I'm at a loss
to describe his going;

something about
a bike in the sky,

a ghost in an unbuttoned raincoat
late for a train.

MEAT IS MURDER

When, overnight, his trade was re-named
in letters daubed five-feet high that bled
down the step and over the pavement,

he stopped hanging those soft stretched bodies,
dew-clawed and raspberry-eyed, their felt ears
lifted on diesel breeze whenever a lorry went by.

The son of a butcher, who was the son
of a butcher's son, he prided himself on brain
and brawn, ruby jewels and red jellies,

a plump pink purse, frisked from a carcass,
tenderly placed beside rib rack and loin.
That morning he gave me a fiver

to peel plastic blood from the glass with a knife,
while he scrubbed shadows from the feet of passers-by,
then sent me for tins of paint for the sill, black gloss

to reflect the times. Years later, I saw him
in the paper, and though I'd known of the gun,
I'd forgotten how, night after night, his moon-face

shone blue in the fly-catcher's light, that sheened
the scrubbed slab and marble counter as he listened
for voices over the refrigerator's hum.

THE PACK

It's useless now, to haul or kick them off; the hare's
already stripped, ribs exposed like an un-clad boat,
and Cassie is belly deep in spattered bluebells.

An ex-racer, her back is marred where they said
a trap fell, though it's likely a lack of insurance
explains the poor stitching.

The hare bolted from tall grass, through the wood,
greyhound and blue-eyed collie following,
blonde Lab and terriers in pursuit.

Now they're blotched, calm, shod with blood.
One terrier shreds a muscled blackberry leg,
the other slathers bone. The collie watches,

nose on stained paws, as the greyhound
shucks the head, peels wet fur, inverts it
like a winter hat, tell-tale ears

rolled clean away. She licks
and shifts the skull with care,
swiftly mouths the brain.

WING

If I'd looked it up later that day
I would have found the hollow bone edge
is called the wrist; that a slope descends
to forewing, that overlapping coverts
are lesser, greater, median, and scapulars are where
the back begins. If I could have looked beyond
the raw, torn joint, and stood at the mouth
of my coppice den, to let it fall open
like a satin fan, I'd have seen
the perfect shoulder of the bastard wing,
full flush secondaries
and mantel of the hind, each quill
blue black and slickly primed.
But what it lacked was all I saw
so I ran, as rooks mocked and raved
in the ruin of trees.

FROM THE BOOK OF CROW ETIQUETTE

To avoid association with a crow's death
feign a limp or otherwise disguise your gait
when passing a crow funeral. In order to escape
a scolding, don't contest a crow's right
to your roof or disrupt its visceral business
among fledglings and eggs. Crows have memories
like wet tar, can recognize the white-stitched ribbon
of a fruitful carrion road, the location of a yard
from which a stone was thrown. Tame crows
give pet names to their keepers; make of this
what you will. Crows that are damaged or ill
are often assisted by others, or else
done in. Decades may pass before a widowed crow
casts the cross of her shadow
on a long abandoned farmyard. A murder might mob
the one-time owner of a slingshot, now
a grandfather in the park. Crows bring gifts
to those who feed them, to children with no prejudice
or fear of crows. You might not need
a stash of broken necklaces, Airfix kit
of sparrow bones, lens cap rinsed in a birdbath,
nor a half heart locket inscribed with 'Best'.
You may not wish for 'friends' to priest a garden fence
or wall, who call before your alarm sounds
and pick at your open dream.

ZOETROPE

Being no twitcher
I can't tell if it's a black swan or cormorant

speeding beside the train, the near-naked trees
interloping

to turn a glimpse of what must be
the most elegant of trajectories

into a zoetrope that strokes
the rooted eye,

wings fully open and now
closed, neck stretched to spear the sky,

and me in the carriage, alone
and transfixed, as far from that bird

as a child, his eye to the slot of a spinning drum
in an empty Victorian nursery.

OYSTERS

Exposure to air would wreck this frame
emerging twenty-two feet
below the Ground Zero excavations.
So the team soak the white oak and hickory keel
that rises through scatterings of animal bone,
ceramic dishes, blue and green bottles
and dozens of shoes, then ferry the timber
to the Earth Observatory,
in Palisades, New York.

The wood is dried slowly in a cold room
then ribs are sliced to match the rings
with signature patterns of living trees
to reveal this ship was most likely built
in seventeen seventy, in a shipyard
near Philadelphia. How clever
we've become, and how resilient
those oysters, their shells
glued tight to the hull.

SARDINES

Perhaps he still dreams that lives and deaths
depend on his attention to the sonar beam
registering an echo from a submarine's hull.

Maybe sweat soaks his night-shirt
as depth and distance are passed
to the bridge, speed and course

altered. Charges are laid, breath held,
and when the sound wave meets itself
the sea erupts. But none of this will surface

during lunch. Instead, O'Hara takes
soundings from Second Avenue, detects
phantoms, submerged, but known to him,

in the same way both he and an artist friend
remember the existence of sardines: a shiver
under a wave of oils, and only their name remaining.

MOROCCO

The glistening bows of a shoal of dolphins
that rise and fall as we watch
from the deck of the Algeciras to Tangier ferry
are always going to pass through here.
So is Stevie Ray, chameleon house pet
of a Berber spice merchant in Essaouira,
tail curled tight as an ammonite
as he slow-mo's from cinnamon
to coriander. And the driver who pilots us
into the Atlas, his liquorish grin
and mirrored shades under a cloud of kif.
He wrestles switchback curves
to a cassette tape of 'One Nation under a Groove'
while two bolts hold the front wheel in place
after a flat on the road out of Marrakesh.
And here's the girl in blue school uniform
and shiny shoes who stands in the bus depot
selling cigarettes, her eyes following mine.

BONJOUR TRISTESSE

Draw the blind on roofs of vein-blue lead.
Your heart will beat through spine, chest, nipple
and neck, send dream down your vertebrae.

Sleep, as morning sun founds an empire
of shadow around the fountains of the Tuileries
while a tide of shutters recedes from patisseries.

The canary's eyes blink open on the balcony,
a stray lifts a leg beside the diplomat's Mercedes
and a bus leaves the depot empty except

for a suspension of motes. Sleep, as nurse's shoes
clap down a polished corridor through the last long breath
of an actress from the sixties, her cheekbones

high under a web of capillaries. Sleep, through
twisting ribbons of coffee, a snowstorm of croissant
flakes, pipes that pulse and vibrate to the shower head.

Sleep, while salesmen yawn in air-conned cars,
as a mop slaps the marble floor of the ministry,
as bottles shoal from bin to dustcart, spilt

like your tears in the head of a lover who
at dawn became an ex, as he climbs the steps
to sit and smoke under a clock of stone.

SYRIA

after Montale

The ancients wrote
that poetry brings you
closer to God. Maybe not
if you're reading mine.
But I knew it was true
the day my voice returned
through a wrap of cloud
as goats rattled from a crag
to cascade across
the road, settling to graze
on blackthorn burs
broom and sedge
while sun and moon
melted and fused,
that day the engine died
and an arrow of blood on a stone
showed the way to Aleppo.

'THIS WOMAN IS ABOUT TO BE VERY LUCKY'

But what is luck on a day when a car explodes
by the stop where she waits for a bus
to take her from a treeless back road
to the missing heart
of the city; a day when the roof of a Fiat Doblo
wings across the sun,
the corrugated fence behind her head
sliced open by a disc brake.
Glass hails onto pavement, a wheel spins
toward the lens.
This is what the voice-over must have meant
by luck; to stand under the arc of debris,
components splayed and smoking
near her sandaled feet, pale insteps
blending at the arches
into milky coffee, her cheeks
rouged by fire, headscarf
lifted in the blast. And make no mistake
this is entertainment; to see a woman in a vortex
as the camera quakes
then settles; to watch her re-emerge
through the muslin of dust,
a scene to be replayed like a miracle.
Each time she'll murmur
what the camera can't catch:
thanks, perhaps, to a god
she might or might not
care to name as she stands
to watch the flames, then turns and walks.

PITY THE ANGELS

having to be there, wherever there is,
disappearing like sunbeams in sea-fret,
mistaken for hallucination from Flanders
to Gaza, from Lampedusa to Aleppo.

It's a tough gig; to be the disembodied
embodiment of solace or love, at the roadside,
say, where an engine still runs, the car on its roof,
a heart pumping until there's nothing left to pump.

Maybe they dream of a new incarnation,
the last affront being another playground
where no one's playing dead, another woman
killed for sex. Or grow careless, drift

from waste ground, leave feathers
that might confuse forensics.
A drone can recognize co-ordinates
but not the family of the bride.

Pupils bloom and shrink, a child learns
to fear the sky. What's an angel to do
but skirt self-pity, know the taking of life
is for the living to decide?

CASSIS

I stop to change my shirt at the top of a track
that runs down to the barn. Sheep stare as the car rolls
to where you're picking blackcurrants. Later, a fire
in a square of bricks, and at midnight, bangers, bottled ale
and the last of a clear spirit you brought back from the East.
A bed of embers glows larval under a feathering of ash
and tomorrow we'll make light work,
prising stalks from glistening blackcurrants,
the long and short cobbled roads of our spines
stooped and aligned, jam-handed
as you funnel sugar through a thick glass neck,
upend vodka to unfurl purple-blue ribbons from the fruit,
steeped and left to ferment for God knows how long,
capped with a bang of your juice-dyed palm.

DIGITS

The Pete Townsend windmill
shattering a lampshade
made of thick glazed pot
when I was drunk and eighteen
was a near thing.
Had the tendons not been
re-joined, what I'd have missed most,
now I think about it,
are the two that I pressed
into the frog-slack spot
under the jaw of a man
whose heart had stopped,
holding them there
for ten long seconds, searching
for a carotid throb.
Nor could I have coaxed rock 'n' roll
from a gut-strung acoustic
at that party where
we watched from the decking
as the sun ran its fingers
through the buzz cut
of a lawn, the chords
inspiring a raft of dawn survivors
into bird-startling song.

IT IS WORTH CONSIDERING LONGEVITY

before bringing home the tortoise who might
out-live you, tender and hairless in its ceramic hull.
Picture him a few weeks after your funeral,
a milky eyelid sliding back to reveal to him
some brave new world of sand-coloured slabs
after decades of cruising a close-cropped lawn.

Consider, also, the juvenile parrot in livid scarlet
and green; imagine him faded as seafront paint,
re-homed, hunkered down in a bird-brained
equivalent of grief, holding his black tongue,
lacking joie de vivre, swearing only when alone.

Ponder, carefully, the purchase of a pencil-sized
corn snake who will grow to the length of a staircase,
the one familiar with the circumference of your neck,
taint of your sweat and temperature of your palm,
now coiled and cold as a curling stone, tongue flickering
the air for a taste of the skin to which no other comes close.

USES OF THE BODY AS A SOURCE FOR ALLEGORY AND METAPHOR

The excavated *skull* of the affair and the built up
head of steam; the *face* of loss, a clock, a cliff; the *teeth*

of cogs, combs, the wind; the *lips* of pitchers, craters
and augers; the *jaws* of mull-grips and dilemmas, not to mention

death; the *tongues* of brogues and ancient Doc Martens;
the *crotches* of arches; the long *arm* of the church

and of boredom; the *armpit* of the paramilitary wing; the *brow*
of the beaten, the hill, of morning; the *breast* made clean; the *skin*

of milk and of a balmy evening; the hard *shoulder* of regret,
the *hair* of the dog and its breadth; the *knuckle* of attraction

and the pierced *nipple* of fate; the long *femur* of the terminally *hip;*
the greased *palm* and the padlocked *heart* of British Steel; the *spine*

of the barn, of stepping stones, of the poem; the *vertebrae*
of e-mail and the *gonads* of vulnerability; the *nose* of the drink,

of the parson, to the grindstone; the *cheeks* in lamé trousers
like two peaches in a solder fountain ; the *ear* to the ground,

the *chest,* the sky; the tender inner *thigh* of expectation;
the *eye* of the storm, the potato and the sunflower;

of the hurricane, the needle, the target, the tiger;
of love, of god, of the beholder.

KNOXVILLE BODY FARM

Better than a box become drum
under a rain of small stones and topsoil

or sent headlong into flame
while some anodyne tune

plays on. Here are undulations
of birdsong, the murmur of milkweed

and long grass, ropes of vapour
trailed by aircraft, fraying into aquamarine.

Insects blow in, lay eggs
in folds of skin. Bones relax in sockets

and someone slips into the lake, a ripple dance
across his face. An end, a shift, a beginning:

the flicker and shimmer of atoms.
Spores dispersed, the tree, fed.

II: *Traces*

ECLIPSE

Outside the ward, nurses and doctors
hold X-rays to the sky. The day turns

cold and blue. Bones rise to the surface of film
the colour of canal water. A crescent sun

lights up fractures: compact, spiral, greenstick,
simple and oblique. The moon is a coin in the neck

of a femur, a shadow on the skull of a window cleaner
who missed a rung. The black ball slips

from arthritic fingers
and through a doorman's jaw.

CARRYING THE ARREST BLEEP

It's cool, at first, to feel it
weighting my pocket, to be wired to a voice
swathed in static,

to run through empty corridors
past a gallery of night-blacked windows,
down stairwells

that smell of the dust
drifting in the hospital's
concrete heart. To be joined

by junior doctors, going hell for leather
over walkways, the city below
sunk in 3am quiet, our feet

skidding in corners, bursting through doors
into the light of a ward
where I'll slap pads

to a chest, get busy with compressions
and the drawing up of drugs.
The buzz wears off

with each heart pumped or shocked;
paper thin skin over prominent ribs,
grey chest hair and deflated breasts

all our futures laid bare
in a strip-lit bay, the whole scene
lasting far too long

and when the registrar asks
if we agree to stop, I meet
his eye, and nod.

STRUCTURES AND PATHWAYS

There's a lot to learn:
how electricity leaps
from node to node;

how chambers fill, expel,
reload. About the crown of arteries
that supply the chest's

clenching fist. Of rhythm
and arrhythmia, frequency,
and dose. How moments

of slowed or blocked flow
equate to cells forever lost.
How to translate the doctor's words

to the patient, the patient's
to the doc. There's a lot to learn
about damage, to learn about cost.

TRACE

My fingers walked
to the fourth intercostal space.
This is where I placed
the first gel-backed tab.
The next went

opposite, across the sternum, on the nipple line.
Easy then to make
a descending arc, attach the leads
until a trace appeared;
the heart. Unlike in films

when it stopped for good
the line was never completely flat,
but wavering like the slap of water
against the dock
long after a boat has passed.

STERILE FIELD

Unpacking latex gloves, saline, cotton wool,
I can't help but ask about the swastika tattoo
inked crudely between thumb and wrist.

'When you' re young, you're stupid'
is all he offers.

I rip a hole in a paper sheet, pass his penis through,
fill the tract from a syringe until its eye leaks lube,
affix the catheter, consider how old ink

might be eclipsed by new; maybe
a Sanskrit mandala, yin and yang motif
or naïve swallow in absolvent blue.

BREAKING THE NEWS

A nightshift can make you
so very tired. But after fighting for
and losing a life, you feel as adrenalized
as you were at nineteen,
driving fast through darkness
before you knew better
on roads you knew blind.
Or lit up with love, those days
before the millennium.

It's a kind of nakedness, to stand
before someone's daughter
or son, hoping they might know
what's to come, might guess
from the look in your eyes.
Take a breath. Offer
your arm. Take a breath.
Offer your help. As if you
didn't feel helpless.

VANISHING ACT

I got used to death
the way you get used
to anything.
I even got used to
the now you see it
now you don't
resurrections, brought about
by chest compressions
and 200 volts;

although not the exit
of a father of four
whose aneurysm burst
mid-joke. I grew familiar
with the heart's erratic magic,
the monitor's drum rolls
and cymbal crashes. A fresh sheet
on an empty bed
after the curtain went back.

I'VE BEEN HIGH

When a Chamois broke from mist
thick as choked bonfire smoke, one hoof
loosening a river of stone. And again, near
Llanberris, spraddled like Spiderman
on the angled slab, twisting a chock
from the crack. A flight above Kent
as an air-cadet, the weald a blur
beneath the wing. But nothing to compare
with level six of this inhospitable monolith,
where, at 4am, there are no furnishings
to soften or mute sounds of life
or death, the sense of altitude
enhanced by jammed on air-con.
The twenty-something doctor
loops a blonde lock behind her ear
as she reviews a drug chart
while I marinade my teeth
in vending machine coke
and the monitors bleep and gong,
the rows of wired hearts
flighty as budgies in a primary school aviary,
alarms alerting us to a change of pace
a stutter or overlong pause, the unsteady pulse
a backdrop to our jokes, our intermittent chat.

BREAK

Assuming a quiet shift, a word
not spoken in case it's a jinx,
there will be time. So choose
the hour you'd prefer
or take what's given. The first
after twelve leaves night
stretching ahead like an unlit beach.

If in luck, you won't hear buzzers,
make a nest on staff-room seats
and sleep, a knock waking you
to dawn light, face creased, tunic stiff
with starch and sweat, a blood-starved patient
being wheeled in, your own heart
drummed by adrenaline.

SHOCKS

When current jolts muscle
my fingers contract. She turns a dial,
asks me to relax, apologises at my first 'ow',
the hand a claw, pincered by voltage.

Electrodes shift to the back of my knee.
I talk to distract myself, say 'I used to work here',
mention I came via the Windsor building, down the corridor
from A&E, past where coronary care once was.

She runs a pulse through my calf, notes
the marionette response, tags flesh above the achilles
to flex the foot. I think of frog's legs,
feel a little sick, remember how the lift

froze between floors, how the man on the trolley
arrested again. Suspended in a metal box,
we shocked him twice, took turns to work his heart,
ten minutes gone before we lurched up the shaft.

AND ANOTHER THING

In films the lips
stay shut.

But in real life
or real death

the jaw drops,
the mouth gapes.

Muscle can't stay tense
in the absence of a pulse.

I just wanted to tell you.

A.M

We leave together, me in wrap-around shades
that set the others laughing. I'm photophobic
I explain, as we step from the lift through lethargic
sliding doors, past a girl in blue pyjamas,
drip-stand in one cannulated hand, cigarette
in the other, cross a mosaic of gum on tarmac
and out of hospital gates, three
shadow-less figures that separate on the corner
while the city exhales the first exhaust of day.
Seven streets to my parked car, across a canal's
creased green V, the wake from swans
that glow through black iron railings,
home to cold sheets and dreamless sleep.

III

THE GREAT ANIMATOR

You manifest in the slap of tarpaulin, wire-song
    in the suspension bridge, a rush of dust
        between border guards' feet.

Destroyer of doldrums, transformer of slender sail
    to pregnant belly, teasing a flag to flight,
        leaving without ceremony.

Courier of playground voices, of pollen
    from stamen to pistil, of flights of swifts –
        their blood still lit by African insects

they stream to summer over village greens.
    Saharan visitor, speckling an Essex windscreen,
        worrying hinge and tile, butting the lintel.

You unload a haul of toads in the town of Ishikawa,
    spill arachnids like un-strung beads
        on the roads of New South Wales.

A God to Hindu and Lakota, you masquerade
    as four stags of Norse myth, the deity
        Fei Lan, sweeping haze-draped Beijing.

You are the opposite of the void, the place
    Simone Weil claimed all sins attempt to fill.
        Yours is the hand

encircling the cool and fevered planet, now holding ash,
    now rain, now hail. Sand twister,
        builder of pyramids,

you stop the eyes and mouths
    of ruined places. Ballerina in her dress
        of smoke, now naked, come to pirouette

among Styrofoam cups and dead cigarettes
    under blurred hospital windows.
        Shepherd of the child's balloon to blue, peeling

a circus poster, swaying daffodils on the grave.
    Meet me again on that ledge where
        arms outstretched I leaned and was held.

WATERLOO TEETH

Wigmakers, jewellers and blacksmiths
all dabbled as dentists, wrenching surrogates
from the jaws of the sugarless poor, fixing rotten grins
with ivory, tacks, and piano wire.

Grave robbers bolstered the enamel supply
until a windfall arrived; Tobacco stained, cracked
or drummer-boy smooth, a harvest from Belgian fields
where soldiers flapped like rooks,

knelt or crouched with string and pliers, moved
from head to head, filling pockets and purses, noses pegged.
Handfuls of nuggets, sorted and sized, tipped
into boiling vats, the ends chopped, each set matched

for colour and shape as if sprung from the gums of a child;
enough, if a cart overturned and spilt its load, to make
a sewer-cleaved street into an ivory road, or turn
parliament's blackened smiles off-white.

SCENT

Description requires a borrowed vocabulary. S*weet* belongs to
    taste, s*harp*
is lifted from touch, and *fruity* is derived from the noun. *Citrus*
    is useless
unless you've smelt citrus. Heavier than air, when wedded to
    memory
scent becomes immortal (see Proust.) Though easy to recall the
    colour
of a lemon, it's harder to conjure its scent. A statue, nose-less,
    entwined
with roses, might remind you to stop and sniff. The olfactory
    bulb expands
until death. Ours is diminutive, compared, say, to a white-eared
    opossum,
European hedgehog or polar bear. Port magnolias and
    hypoglycaemic breath
arrive at the brain as pear drops or nail varnish. The violet is
    famous
for its fleeting grace. Tiger's urine resembles fragrant basmati,
    but of this
only zookeepers are aware. Hunters can't tell buck from doe;
    many killed
are the wrong gender for musk. Ambergris is derived from a
    fatty hairball
expelled from a sperm whale's oesophagus. A coin, the world
    over, is redolent
of blood. A pheromone spray, bought from a vending machine
    in a public toilet,
contains porcine gland extract, liable to attract lonely pigs.

NYMPHEA THERMARUM STOLEN FROM PRINCESS OF WALES CONSERVATORY, KEW GARDENS.

Squads of kids in high-vis vests
trek past lurid bromeliads, vertiginous cacti
breathing desert cool, fibrous mangroves
and red *Passiflora,* vibrant in forest heat.

They squeal as a beetle skitters a walkway,
while Duncan, the apprentice, measures levels
in the ponds. He checks the rarest, most
endangered lily in the world, white buds at the foot

of a concrete bridge. 'Twenty-three,' he says aloud;
there's no need to recount, nothing but a hole
where the twenty fourth should be.
Someone snaked along a railway sleeper, parted

the *Anthuriums,* balanced above mud
to scoop out the minute lily. The lad sprints off
to get his boss. Now Johnson stands on the bridge,
spots digit prints in the hand-shaped divert.

He's been unsettled for weeks, finding
two St Helena ebonies for sale on the web.
"Screw you," the seller had said
"this is capitalism, and you know it."

He thinks a search might be ridiculous,
weary of saving the world, one plant
at a time. The alert goes out; has anyone
seen a man with a muddy hand?

Forensics arrive, zip white suits
and crawl into beds, magnifying glasses
strapped to their heads.

THE GLASS DELUSION

It peaked, or so scholars think,
in medieval times; a notable example being
the sixth King Charles, who wrapped himself in rugs
to prevent his buttocks from shattering.

In a story by Cervantes, the hero, poisoned
by a quince, feels he is made of glass.
People who believe they are glass
avoid parties, the opera, and any

kind of crowd. Asylum documents record
three hundred women with legs and arms and hearts
fragile and transparent. Some explained
their backs, heads, and even dreams

were composed of glass. Recently, in Paris,
a young man gestured to the window and asked
what do you see? The psychologist listed
window box, red tulips, a dog walker, parked cars.

But Dr. you've missed the glass. You didn't
see it, but it's there. That's me; there and not.
Darling, lately, I've been wondering about us.

BEER GARDEN

On the bench where we'd run out of words
a wasp clung to a glass and throbbed
as if honey ran back and forth
in the sugar-spun thorax.

It crawled up the froth-laced wall
like some winged samurai, survivor
of a great battle, still capable of wounding,
drawn to the lip to taste, overreach, fall.

THE FAITHLESS HUSBAND

(after Lorca)

She took me to the river
when the windows of the houses
were quiet and black
and her sandals whispered in the grass
as dogs barked by the path.

We left the halo of Lucozade lights
and the Milky Way hung like dust,
passed blackberry bushes,
cans and bottles in sleeves of ash,
a train of white plastic
snagged on hawthorn,
a concertina of Rizlas
lying open in the grass.

In a meadow on the river's lip
she rolled the straps from her shoulders
and I heard the fall of cotton
among buttercups and dandelions.
A tongue of blood flickered my palm
as she pressed my hand
against her breast.
I too undressed, her first touch lighter
than the breezes of July.

The knot I undid
and lifted from her nape
was softer than silk, the curve
of her belly
smooth as sun-warmed marble,
her eyes full of fire.

That night I looked up
at the wingtip lights of jets
that scrawled gently over sleeping heads
and steel that sheathed glass
tearing cloud above the Warf.

Smudged with soil and dew
stained with crushed green blades
and salted with each other,
we left the river silver-plated with light,
the purple iris swaying
with the weight of a butterfly.

After bacon, eggs and coffee,
we browsed antiques, or bric-a-brac
and I bought her three pictures
framed in pine; a blear of field poppies,
a phalanx of lavender, a spiral coil
of red rose briar.

I didn't fall in love that night,
or call again, and she asked
for nothing but my name
when she took me to the river.

DRESS

I'm at my desk when she comes to ask
if I'll do up her newly-sewn dress. So I turn from my stitching
and un-stitching of words

to where she smooths her tulip hips, the zip ready to run
between my thumb and finger, to purse
a seam of satin

from the hollow of her back
to the base on her neck, to swallow her warm white
freckled V.

IN THE BIG HOUSE

Anyone would think this lemon-lit September
would last forever, as a pendulum tocks
in the Brasso scented hall, while in the lounge
thin teacups clink saucers
and the lady in a red flowered dress exclaims
Oh, girl! even though my mum
is not a girl. I'll search these high rooms
for the bell-collared cat, hum
'Crocodile Rock' and think of Jesus
on a fishing boat. No one would believe
any of this could ever be interrupted;
but the handsome son
whose photo's on the piano
is going to be killed in a war
and any moment now
in the sun-drowned conservatory
a row of bloody beads
will spring from my cheek
at the sweep of a tabby's paw.

RISOTTO

She wouldn't believe it; the saffron
nearly five quid: a lot of lira for a pinch
of dried stigmas, even if they are handpicked,
packed in a tangerine tinted plastic box,

inserted like a ship into a bottle, the only one left
in the rack at the Co-op, those auburn strands
the colour of spice-up-your-Christmas hair dye
or the plucked legs of an exotic insect.

Only the packaging is different; her zafferano
arrived in paper packets with a crocus on the side.
Still, worth it, I think, for a glaze of sunshine.
The rice is Arborio, from Piedmont, or Pidemonte

as she would say, short grain, pearl-like,
a member of the grass family, the same
as all rice, but not. At home, I soften
more unsalted butter than is good for me,

slide in fine chopped onion, then the riso
and a glass of white wine, though she'd have sploshed
the red that was always open. Now, the simmering stock,
piano, piano. a ladle at a time.

BACK TO BLACK

Success, whatever it was, whatever
you thought it was, stuck its tongue
in your mouth, undressed you swiftly,
had its way, and left. The accolades
need not have led you to emptiness,

smashed on a cocktail of insecurity
and conceit: or soured your breath,
lay down on your voice the way
an LA heat-haze lays down
to smother morning breeze.

Nor pulled you into lights
that left you looking into black,
an audience out there somewhere
gazing back, heads level with your feet.

ACCIDENTAL MUSIC

We played in different registers. Undertones
merged with overtones. Mostly, we made
a cacophony.

Often, one would veer away,
only to return and play
their new favourite solo.

Passages entwined. Chords merged
and broke. Each lived in performance
or rehearsal. And sometimes

we made music: the strangest,
most untamed, most unnameable music.

NEW MODEL VILLAGE

Each house once held a family; the man
maybe an opener for the cricket team
or one who limped home from the pit
with a crook back and worn-out knees:
the Dad who winked and fished for a coin
to buy a quarter of sweets; who, after his bath,
lifted children so their shadows filled the wall.
Or one who never laughed, face
dark as the peak, eyes, always coal.

And daughters who dreamed of boys
to bring them posies from the hill;
men who'd not get sick from drink,
grow generous with their fists, or both.
A man who'd not crack like a prop shaft;
the kind a woman might love enough
to rise like a lark over red-bricked yards,
lines of shirts, long-johns, a pinafore dress,
the blown bow of her camisole, cupping April hail.

WOODLOUSE

He stops typing when a minute armadillo
undulates over the keys; slides paper
under its feet, turns the sheet
as if it's alight, while the louse climbs
against gravity, flaps it from the open window
into space. He thinks of other
household parasites;
silverfish with tapered abdomens,
so agile and afraid of light, a filmy clot
that split and vanished when exposed.
Thankfully, he's not seen one for years
but remembers a damp
under-sink cupboard in Greenwich
where roaches clock-worked out across the tiles,
a sight he'd denied and shut
away, much as he did
with something he can't talk about:
but he was a child then
and doesn't dwell on it.

ERA

No crack deals, walls blotched with damp
or a stabbing in a stairwell. Just the sun
wrapping gold around the highest windows,
laundry, flagging balconies
and Lily with the bandaged legs
handing boiled sweets from a doorway.

Shadows deep as swimming pools
brought goose bumps to flesh
under the long arm of a walkway, the big ship at sail
down the alley-alley-oh, as concrete got hot
in the summer-flooded quad
and the soles of Start-Rite sandals
kissed and left the planet, a skipping rope, ticking time.

AMMONITE

Who found that fossil
in the fallen face
on a rain-softened day?

Was it me or my sister
who chose that rock
below a Cornish cliff,

lifting and dropping it
to split and unlock
a frozen honey spiral?

Whose high voice carried
on salt-loaded wind
to bring Dad back across the beach?

He's kneeling to chip it free,
a perfect crystal coil.
In my head

it was always me
but you told it differently
and lately,

though I don't
know why, I've begun
to believe you.

WEDDING VIDEO

The bells vie with thunder
while we swap kisses, handshakes, jokes.
Then my sister shelters underneath his coat
and they run into rain that falls hard as rice.

She wipes misted glass with her ringed hand,
blows a kiss to the lens and waves goodbye.
I follow the Jag with its dancing cans
until it turns into the road and out of sight,

pan back to those faces, familiar bones
exposed in a flash of light.

SLUMBERLAND

Wrestled downstairs against its will,
folded and flopped into a skip
along with all the nights
we breathed each other in,
along with whatever remains
of dreams, tears, baby milk,
a thousand little deaths.

I read how each mattress gains
in weight, made fat by dead skin
and slow or breakneck sweat,
our images preserved in fabric
over concertinaed springs
like those eiderdowns of volcanic ash
that mould and keep the shapes of sleep.

THE RED FOREST

What they give you
in controlled doses
shrinks the brains of birds.

Bees and spiders
fail to thrive
and there are few butterflies.

Nothing happens
quickly. A trunk lies
in thick leaf litter, untouched

but for a shifting tattoo
of ants. Microbes and fungi
have nearly all died out,

so trees grow slow and slant. We too
advance slowly, trying to hold on
to the idea of your going.

THAW

The boy leaves a kiss on her forehead
and I take him to wait by a patch of snow
that's losing its grip on gravel.

A blackbird alarms in the ivy.
Our breath comes in linen wisps.
Ice-water buds along the eves.

He balances on a low wall, machine-gunning baddies,
becomes a superhero. Beyond the laurel
two men walk dogs.

By the window, you perch on the electric bed
in a wedge of sunlight, one hand over
your mother's. I read your lips;

how about a little ice-cream?
She nods, though both of you know
it'll melt untouched while she sleeps.

NIGHT SWIMMING

for Joan Hewitt

That August day was weirdly lit: heat built,
lawns turned the purple of Welsh slate
and a forecast storm

never came. Bees trod pollen-loaded
blooms, a butterfly opened
in the sunflower's eye, voices drifted from a room

where writers wandered toward themselves.
That evening, you said *let's swim*, so we met
at midnight below the castle on the rock

where I waded the path of the moon, laid my cheek
to the cold black, kicked and stroked home.

BOWES ROAD

I'd never seen rats run on cables before
nor heard windows vibrate to the throb of HGVs.
Jim was a native, toured his manor like a lord,

car stereo booming *I Wanna Be Adored*
from the heart of Haringey to its borders.
One Saturday, bushes appeared,

lifted from the rich soil of some leafy suburb:
a chance haul, bagged and stacked into the boot,
bedded in the thin margins of the yard, stout roots

firmed and watered. Jim had faith in their future,
though neither I nor the girl whose kiss we'd shared
believed it when blood red buds unfurled.

Our triangle collapsed with the Berlin Wall;
summer gone, and one livid bloom hung on, defying
a lead-soaked breeze that blew from the North Circular.

CALLER

A soft thump on the glass
made me look up from my desk.

On the roof
a sparrow, concussed in the furrow
of terracotta tiles.

He'd hit the window
hard, sat blinking in a downy drift
as if the world was new.

I worried for his jigged spine
the knuckle of his skull
and thought of you

in your helmet and leathers.
He tilted his eye
to mine, puffed his chest and flew.

AFTER THE GALLERY

Heading north again, yellow and orange leaves stream past
like dots freed from a Seurat painting.

We pass a plump brown river, the promise of another flood
held under its skin.

A horse in a green coat
rolls in a field; a wash of mist

softens a ridge. Outside Chesterfield
I try to look away from a girl

who studies the Highway Code.
You're almost old, my eyes tell

the tunnel-blacked window.
She glances up

and through me, serene and assured
as a Leonardo.

BEYOND NORTH

I'd go there too, if all I'd known
was warped or riven,
to a place of un-diluted light
where the wind comes naked
after its flight across the sea.
I could work, building hatches
to batten, break firewood open
on the blade of an axe, slap up
gull-splattered stone
in a new coat of white.
I'd throw grain for the all-important chickens,
majestic in their suits of henna and rust,
their feet lifted high and placed
so carefully, as if the grass
might hurt. I understand that
the language of rain is common,
and that snow is often spoken,
particularly at night. I'd like to wake
to the silence of still waves,
white horses hitched and rock tethered
under a sky of ice.

WILL

Son, I'd rather leave you the memory of the day
we cycled to Mevagissy
than these shelved books and racks of clothes
that carry the trace of my scent.
Two swans rode their reflections around
the double harboured wall
as rust-hulled fishing boats rose
on the swell. That night at Jodrell Bank
astronomers watched Ison speed sunward
with a snowball's chance in hell.
None could quite believe
its re-emergence, the brilliance of the new tail.

NOTES

Knoxville Body Farm is a research facility in Tennessee. Set up to study human decomposition, it relies on the donation of bodies to continue its work.

'Back to Black' is the title of a song and album by the late singer, Amy Winehouse.

The Red Forest is the name given to an area surrounding the Chernobyl Nuclear Power Plant. It is derived from the ginger-brown colour of the pine trees that died following absorption of radiation after the accident at the reactor in April 1986.